HAL•LEONARD

Pro Vocal®

BETTER THAN KARAOKE!

VOLUME 12

Ella Fitzgerald

MW00365412

Cover Photo: Photofest

ISBN 978-1-4234-5364-2

HAL•LEONARD®
CORPORATION

7777 W. BLUEMOUND RD. P.O. BOX 13819 MILWAUKEE, WI 53213

For all works contained herein:
Unauthorized copying, arranging, adapting, recording or public performance
is an infringement of copyright.
Infringers are liable under the law.

Visit Hal Leonard Online at
www.halleonard.com

Ella Fitzgerald

CONTENTS

Don't Be That Way

By Benny Goodman, Mitchell Parish and Edgar Sampson

Copyright © 1938 by Robbins Music Corporation
Rights for the U.S. Extended Renewal Term Controlled by Ragbag Music Publishing Corporation (ASCAP),
Parmit Music and EMI Robbins Music Corporation
All Rights for Ragbag Music Publishing Corporation Administered by Jewel Music Publishing Co., Inc.
International Copyright Secured   All Rights Reserved
Used by Permission

Don'cha Go 'Way Mad

Words and Music by Al Stillman, Jimmy Mundy and Illinois Jacquet

Intro
Light Jazz Swing

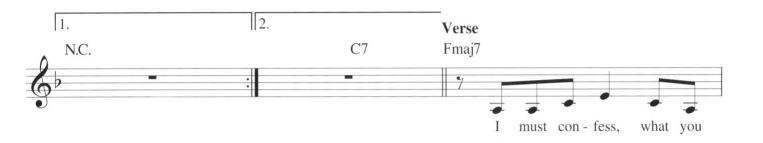

I must con-fess, what you

say is true. ___ I had a ren-dez-vous with some-bod-y new.

It's the on-ly one I ev-er had. ___ Ba-by, ba-by, don-'cha

go 'way ___ mad. ___ Cheat-in' shows, and it nev-er goes. ___

You have a rea-son to be mad, I sup-pose. He was on-ly just

© 1950 ADVANCED MUSIC CORP.
© Renewed 1978 RYTVOC, INC. and WARNER BROS. INC.
All Rights Reserved

It's Only a Paper Moon

Lyric by Billy Rose and E.Y. "Yip" Harburg
Music by Harold Arlen

Intro

Medium Jazz Swing

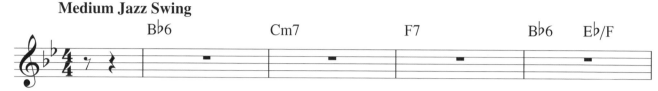

Verse

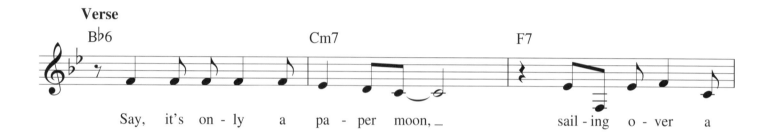

Say, it's on-ly a pa-per moon, __ sail-ing o-ver a

card-board sea. But it would-n't be make - be - lieve __ if you __

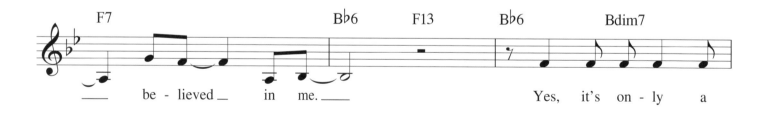

__ be - lieved __ in me. __ Yes, it's on-ly a

can - vas sky, __ hang-ing o-ver a mus - lin tree. __

© 1933 (Renewed) CHAPPELL & CO., GLOCCA MORRA MUSIC and S.A. MUSIC CO.
All Rights for GLOCCA MORRA MUSIC Administered by NEXT DECADE ENTERTAINMENT, INC.
All Rights Reserved

But it would-n't be make — be-lieve _ if you _ be-lieved _ in me. _

Bridge

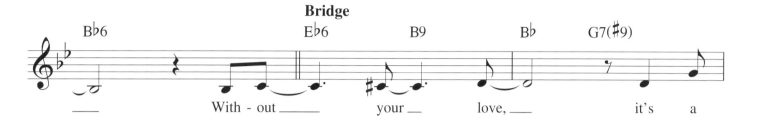

_ With-out _____ your _ love, _____ it's a

hon-ky-tonk _ pa-rade. _ With-out _____ your love, _

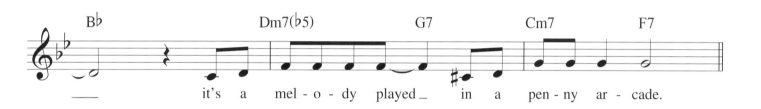

_ it's a mel-o-dy played _ in a pen-ny ar-cade.

Verse

It's a Bar-num and Bai-ley world, _ just as _____ pho-ny

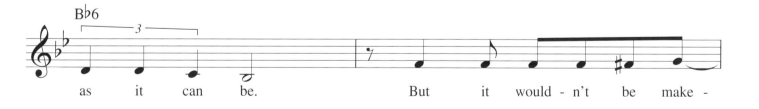

as it can be. But it would-n't be make -

— be-lieve _ if you _ be-lieved _ in me. _____

Instrumental

32

Verse

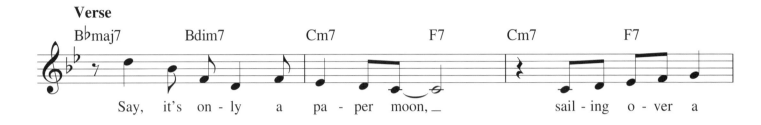

Say, it's on - ly a pa - per moon, __ sail - ing o - ver a

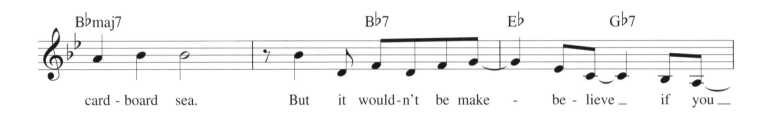

card - board sea. But it would-n't be make - be - lieve __ if you __

__ be - lieved __ in me. __ Yes, __ it's on - ly a can -

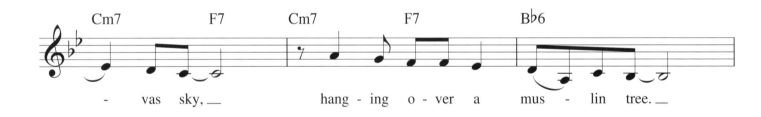

- vas sky, __ hang - ing o - ver a mus - lin tree. __

But it would-n't be make - be - lieve __ if you __ be - lieved __ in me.

Bridge

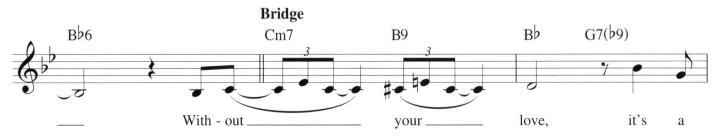

__ With - out _____ your _____ love, it's a

14

hon - ky - tonk — pa - rade.   With - out ___ your love, —

___   it's a mel - o - dy played in a pen - ny ar - cade.

Verse

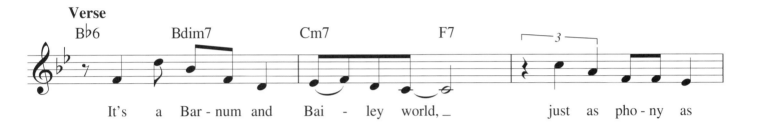

It's a Bar - num and Bai - ley world, —   just as pho - ny as

it can be. ___   But it would - n't be make - be - lieve _ if you —

Outro

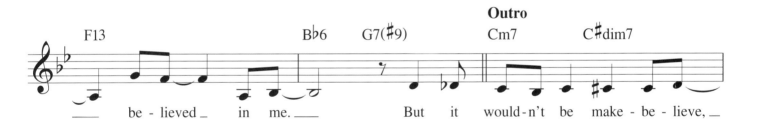

___ be - lieved _ in me. ___   But it would - n't be make - be - lieve, —

___ be - lieve _ if you ___ be - lieved _ in me. ___

___

Misty

Words by Johnny Burke
Music by Erroll Garner

Intro

Slow Jazz Ballad

Look at _____ me, I'm as

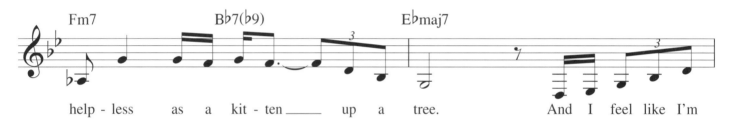

help - less as a kit - ten _____ up a tree. And I feel like I'm

cling - ing to a cloud. ___ I can't un - der - stand, I

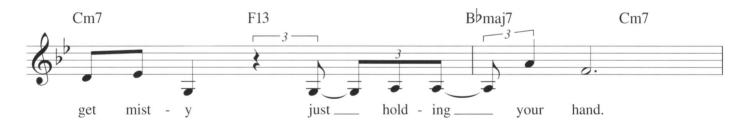

get mist - y just ____ hold - ing _____ your hand.

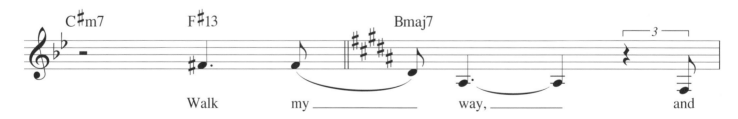

Walk my _____ way, _____ and

Copyright © 1955 by Octave Music Publishing Corp., Marke Music Publishing Co., Inc.,
Reganesque Music, Limerick Music and My Dad's Songs, Inc.
Copyright Renewed 1982
All Rights for Marke Music Publishing Co., Inc. Administered by Universal Music - MGB Songs
All Rights for Reganesque Music, Limerick Music and My Dad's Songs, Inc. Administered by Spirit Two Music, Inc.
International Copyright Secured   All Rights Reserved

a thou - sand __ vi - o - lins __ be - gin to play. Or it might be the

sound __ of your hel - lo. __ That mu - sic I hear, I

get mist - y __ the mo - ment you're __ near. __

Bridge

Can't you see that you're lead - ing me on? __

And it's just what I want __ you to do.

Don't you no - tice how hope - less - ly I'm lost? __

That's __ why I'm fol - low - ing you.

'Round Midnight

Words by Bernie Hanighen
Music by Thelonious Monk and Cootie Williams

Intro-Verse
Very Slowly

It be - gins to tell 'round mid - night, mid - night.

I do pret - ty well 'til af - ter sun - down.

Sup - per - time, I'm feel - in' sad, but

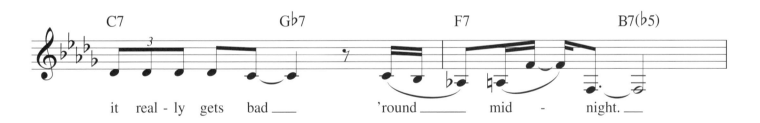

it real - ly gets bad 'round mid - night.

Mem - 'ries al - ways start 'round mid - night.

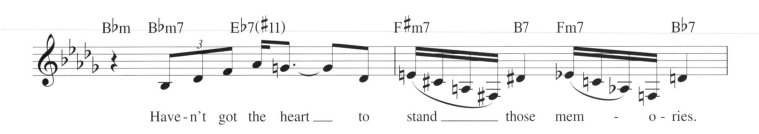

Have-n't got the heart to stand those mem - o - ries.

Copyright © 1944 (Renewed 1971) by Thelonious Music Corp. and Warner Bros. Inc.
International Copyright Secured   All Rights Reserved

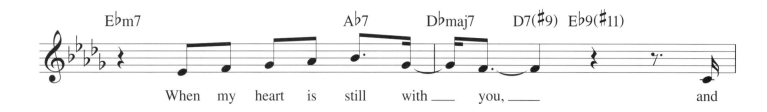

When my heart is still with ___ you, ___ and

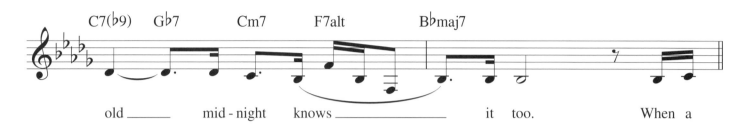

old ___ mid - night knows ___ it too. When a

Bridge

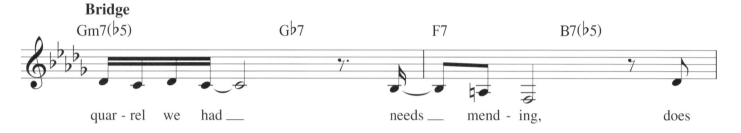

quar - rel we had ___ needs ___ mend - ing, does

it mean ___ that our love ___ is end - ing? ___

Dar - lin', I need you. ___ Late - ly I find ___ you're ___

___ out of ___ my ___ heart, and ___ I'm ___ out of my mind. ___

Verse

___ Let our hearts ___ take ___ wing ___ 'round mid - night, ___ mid - night.

Let the an - gels sing ____ for your ____ re - turn - ing,

'til our love is safe ____ and sound, ____ and ____

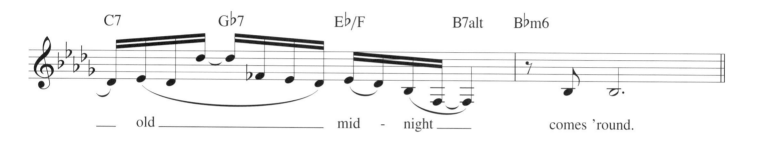

____ old ____ mid - night ____ comes 'round.

Outro
Freely

Feel - in' sad, real - ly gets bad

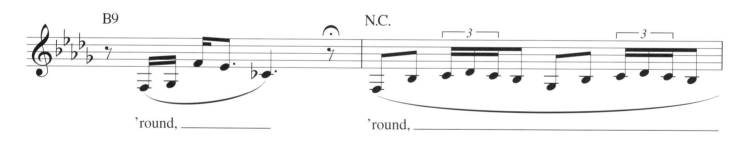

'round, ____ 'round, ____

'round ____

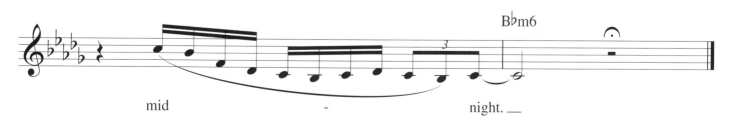

mid - night. ____

A-Tisket, A-Tasket

Words and Music by Ella Fitzgerald and Van Alexander

© 1938 (Renewed) EMI ROBBINS CATALOG INC.
All Rights Controlled by EMI ROBBINS CATALOG INC. (Publishing) and ALFRED PUBLISHING CO., INC. (Print)
All Rights Reserved   Used by Permission

- et. She was truck-in' on down the av - e - nue,

not a sin - gle thing __ to do. __ She went peck - peck - peck - in' all __

___ a - round, __ when she spied it on ___ the ground. __ She

took it, she took it, __ my lit - tle yel - low bas -

- ket. __ And if she does - n't bring __ it back, _ I

think that I _____ will die.

Interlude

10

A -

Verse

tis - ket, a - tas - ket, I lost my yel - low bas -

Bridge

What Is There to Say

Lyrics by E.Y. "Yip" Harburg
Music by Vernon Duke

Intro
Very Freely

Verse

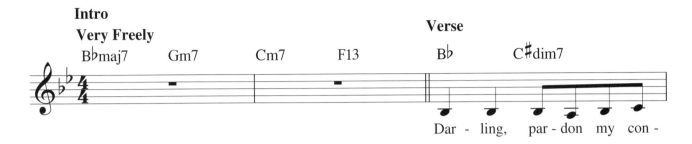

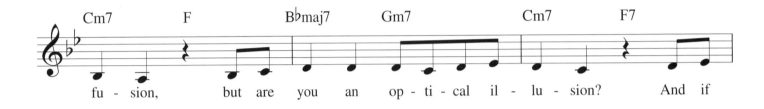

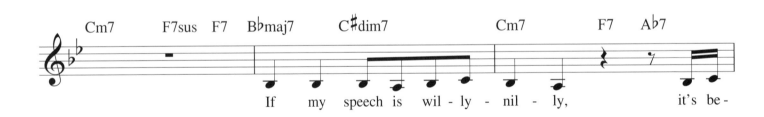

Copyright © 1933 by Kay Duke Music and Glocca Morra Music
Copyright Renewed
All Rights for Kay Duke Music Administered by Universal Music - MGB Songs
All Rights for Glocca Morra Music Administered by Next Decade Entertainment, Inc.
International Copyright Secured   All Rights Reserved

You're an Old Smoothie

Words by B.G. DeSylva
Music by Richard A. Whiting and Nacio Herb Brown

© 1932 (Renewed) WB MUSIC CORP.
All Rights for the Extended Renewal Term in the U.S. Controlled by WB MUSIC CORP., STEPHEN BALLENTINE MUSIC
and THE SONGWRITERS GUILD OF AMERICA
All Rights for the World outside of the U.S. Controlled by WB MUSIC CORP.
All Rights Reserved   Used by Permission

Pro Vocal® Series
SONGBOOK & SOUND-ALIKE CD
SING 8 CHART-TOPPING SONGS WITH A PROFESSIONAL BAND

Whether you're a karaoke singer or an auditioning professional, the Pro Vocal® series is for you! Unlike most karaoke packs, each book in the ProVocal Series contains the lyrics, melody, and chord symbols for eight hit songs. The CD contains demos for listening, and separate backing tracks so you can sing along. The CD is playable on any CD player, but it is also enhanced so PC and Mac computer users can adjust the recording to any pitch without changing the tempo! Perfect for home rehearsal, parties, auditions, corporate events, and gigs without a backup band.

BROADWAY SONGS
00740247 Women's Edition.................................$12.95
00740248 Men's Edition.....................................$12.95

MICHAEL BUBLÉ
00740362 ....$14.95

CHRISTMAS STANDARDS
00740299 Women's Edition.................................$12.95
00740298 Men's Edition.....................................$12.95

KELLY CLARKSON
00740377 ....$14.95

PATSY CLINE
00740374 ....$14.95

CONTEMPORARY HITS
00740246 Women's Edition.................................$12.95
00740251 Men's Edition.....................................$12.95

DISCO FEVER
00740281 Women's Edition.................................$12.95
00740282 Men's Edition.....................................$12.95

DISNEY'S BEST
00740344 Women's Edition.................................$14.95
00740345 Men's Edition.....................................$14.95

DISNEY FAVORITES
00740342 Women's Edition.................................$14.95
00740343 Men's Edition $14.95

'80S GOLD
00740277 Women's Edition.................................$12.95
00740278 Men's Edition.....................................$12.95

ELLA FITZGERALD
00740378..$14.95

GREASE
00740369 Women's Edition.................................$14.95
00740370 Men's Edition.....................................$14.95

JOSH GROBAN
00740371 ....$17.95

HIGH SCHOOL MUSICAL 1 & 2
00740360 Women's Edition.................................$14.95
00740361 Men's Edition.....................................$14.95

HANNAH MONTANA
00740375 ....$14.95

HIP-HOP HITS
00740368 Men's Edition.....................................$14.95

HITS OF THE '70S
00740384 Women's Edition.................................$14.95
00740383 Men's Edition $14.95

JAZZ BALLADS
00740353 Women's Edition.................................$12.95

JAZZ FAVORITES
00740354 Women's Edition.................................$12.95

JAZZ STANDARDS
00740249 Women's Edition.................................$12.95
00740250 Men's Edition.....................................$12.95

JAZZ VOCAL STANDARDS
0074037 Women's Edition...................................$14.95

Prices, contents, & availability subject to change without notice.
Disney charaters and artwork © Disney Enterprises, Inc.

FOR MORE INFORMATION, SEE YOUR LOCAL MUSIC DEALER, OR WRITE TO:

HAL•LEONARD®
CORPORATION
7777 W. BLUEMOUND RD. P.O. BOX 13819 MILWAUKEE, WI 53213

Visit Hal Leonard online at www.halleonard.com

MOVIE SONGS
00740365 Women's Edition.................................$14.95
00740366 Men's Edition.....................................$14.95

MUSICALS OF BOUBLIL & SCHÖNBERG
00740350 Women's Edition.................................$14.95
00740351 Men's Edition.....................................$14.95

ELVIS PRESLEY
00740333 Volume 1 ....$14.95
00740335 Volume 2 ....$14.95

R&B SUPER HITS
00740279 Women's Edition.................................$12.95
00740280 Men's Edition.....................................$12.95

FRANK SINATRA CLASSICS
00740347 ....$14.95

FRANK SINATRA STANDARDS
00740346 ....$14.95

TORCH SONGS
00740363 Women's Edition.................................$12.95
00740364 Men's Edition.....................................$12.95

TOP HITS
00740380 Women's Edition.................................$14.95

ANDREW LLOYD WEBBER
00740348 Women's Edition.................................$14.95
00740349 Men's Edition.....................................$14.95

WEDDING GEMS
00740309 Book/CD Pack Women's Edition $12.95
00740310 Book/CD Pack Men's Edition.................$12.95
00740311 Duets Edition $12.95

HANK WILLIAMS
00740386 ....$14.95

03C